MATH 009

Mutinies

I0407883

Maritime Anthropology (MATH) a topic which covers prehistoric, historic and modern life, and inspirations derived from the world's oceans and the brave souls who have subsisted on and inhabited the surrounding environs of the sea.

MATH 009 Mutinies focuses on the people and events that led to a sense of injustice, and the drastic measure in which sailors exist in which a mutiny must be called. Laws on the seas, and the judicial organizations which develop and adhere to those laws.

Research and module development

by

Yvonne-Cher Skye

Skye Research

Copyright 2017

Skye Research

an affiliate of Your Girl Friday International

Black Rose Communications,

111 S. 35th St.

San Diego, California 92113

Statement of Purpose

To create an educational program from which educators can create a program to sell to potential students as part of a maritime cultural experience. The intended audience can be variable from a one hour, one day seminar course to an 18 week course semester.

The actual lesson plans are at the discretion of the instructor. The materials available in this booklet are meant to be a reference point to assist the instructor in developing a foundation from which the intended course can be derived.

As this is in the early stages of production, all comments and suggestions for improvement are welcome.

Sincerely,

Yvonne-Cher Skye

Table of Contents

Summary

Objective:

Lecture on mutinies throughout maritime history: ranging from the infamous Mutiny on the Bounty to Hermione, and specific focus on mutinies that occurred in local regions.

Materials Needed:

Instructor: PowerPoint Presentation

Students: Journals, writing implements

Vocabulary introduced:

- Batavia Wreck
- HMS Bounty
- HMS Hermione
- Spithead and Note
- Press Gang

Background:

All of Maritime History began with the observation of the oceans and rivers by man.

Further specific lectures can be assigned module letters as the need arises.

Reference:

Seafaring Lore and Legend, Peter D. Jeans 2007

Wikipedia

Personal experiences

Personal research

Lesson Plan:

Introduce the terms and concepts via PowerPoint by using images and bulleted lists to convey the information. Dialogue with the students in a question and answer format.

Introduction:

Explain subject matter, and resource materials, with an eye on multimedia and hands-on instruction when materials are available.

Body:

- Batavia Wreck
- HMS Bounty

- HMS Hermione
- Spithead and Note
- Press Gang

Conclusion:

Direction on how instructor can conclude the module

Clean-Up:

Students take their things with them.

Learning sessions

Textbook reading chapters can be developed per the Instructor's chosen textbook or via their own manual dependent on scope of material intended to be covered in this course

Individual sections with dividers each focusing on one component of the content: All of the following will be determined by Instructor, module course outline gives examples of the following:

  a. Learning outcomes

  b. Session Information

  c. Learning activities

  d. Learning Resources

  e. Evaluation Procedures

  f. Timing and assignment

Course Outline

Catalog number: MATH 009   **Course Title:** Mutinies

Year: 2017   **Semester:** Spring

Instructor: **Office Location:**

Office Hours:

Objectives of the course:

Explain mutinies and conditions that lead up to mutinies

Famous mutinies, their captains, and lead mutineer

Punishment and Maritime Laws Past and Present

Any measurable objectives that can be demonstrated by student.

Procedures for accomplishing these objectives:

Lectures

Class discussions

Analytic questions

Projects

Research papers

Use of visual and oral reports

Fields trips

Visiting lecturers

Student testimonials

Use of multimedia i.e. videos, audio recordings to exemplify topics

Student requirements for completion of the course:

Varies per instructor discretion and length of program

During introductory lecture, the instructor must list specific work students must complete in order to receive credit for the course

Student need to demonstrate the accomplishment of each objective, examples are as follows:

Read all the chapters in the textbook

Submit a research paper

Oral report on topic

Submit book report

Complete lab reports

Complete periodic quizzes

Complete mid-term exam

Complete final exam

Grading Practices:

Students will be graded using above methods, at the instructor's discretion

Relative importance of each item

Four quizzes: 40%

Two book reports 20%

Term paper 20%

Final exam 20%

Equals 100%

Rules Concerning student absence and lateness:

At the discretion of the instructor and student agreement

If marina, ship or school follows specific rules, then state explicitly

Textbook:

List author, title publisher, date of publication of any required texts, manuals

Weekly Outline Topics to be covered:

List topics in sequential order

The Batavia Wreck and Mutiny

HMS Bounty Mutiny

HMS Hermione Mutiny

Spithead and the Nore Mutiny

The Press Gang

List tests, quizzes, due dates for papers

Audio Visual Materials to be used:

List any visual elements to be used during course including:

PowerPoint presentations

Youtube videos

Photos

Graphs

Maps

List of supplementary readings:

MATH 009 Glossary

List books, periodicals, articles which students should read in addition to text

Miscellaneous information:

Any information that will further clarify what is hoped to be achieved in the course and how you plan to achieve it.

Audio Visual Experience

Photos

Please see attached document entitled Photos.

These will be updated as research is continued.

Useful weblinks leading to images can be found on the following websites:

Websites on subject

http://www.merriam-webster.com/dictionary/archetype

https://skyeresearchygfi.wordpress.com/2016/06/09/math-marine-anthropology-009-summary/

https://skyeresearchygfi.wordpress.com/2016/09/03/math-009-youtube-channel/

Audio recordings, videos or script to explain each section

Youtube channel Playlist MATH 001 at this link:

https://www.youtube.com/playlist?

list=PLBHbcZSn310CUhmMTkHoPqJIylPpYwiJr

Topics

Batavia Wreck

HMS Bounty

HMS Hermoine

HMS Marie Antoinette

Keil Mutiny

Nore Mutiny

San Antonio

Spithead Mutiny

SS Columbia Eagle

These topics correspond with the notes and discussion plans that are available upon request.

Appendices

    Glossary

    Maps

    Artistic renderings

    Works Cited

Glossary

B

Batavia Wreck – In 1647, Captain Delsaert was mutined against by Jeronimus.

C

Captain – a leader in command of a passenger or merchant ship.

Commander - a leader who ranks below all the following: Rear Admiral, a Captain, and a Commodore.

Commodore – a leader who ranks above a Rear Admiral, a Captain, and a Commander.

D

De Cartagena, Juan - was the Captain of the *San Antonio* mutineer in 1520 against Ferdinand Magellan. One of two men that were marooned as a result.

De La Reina, Pero Sanchez – mutineer in 1520 against Ferdinand Magellan. One of two men that were marooned as a result.

G

Glatkowski, Alvin – mutineer on the SS Columbia Eagle – March 1970 Mutiny on an American ship during the Vietnam War. Lead by Clyde McKay and him.

H

HMS Bounty – in 1789, Captain William Bligh, was mutinied against by Fletcher Christian

HMS Hermione – Bloodiest mutiny in British Naval history. Captain Pigot on 21 Sept. 1797 his crew mutinied due to his cruelty and the death of their shipmate on his orders.

HMS Marie Antoinette – was built in the United Kingdom in 1793. The mutiny occurred 27 Dec 1797 and the mutineers sailed her to a French Port in the West Indies.

Hudson, Henry – Captain of the *Discovery*, a mutiny occurred in 1611 while he was searching for the Northwest Passage.

K

Kiel Mutiny – in Germany October 1918, several ships were involved mutinies were in response to unfair work conditions and wages. Started German revolution which ended World War I.

M

Magellan, Ferdinand 1520 circumnavigated the globe. Mutiny against him by Captain Juan De Cartagena Captain of the *San Antonio*, and Pero Sanchez De La Reina. Ferdinand marooned the two men, and neither were ever seen or heard from again.

Mutineer – a person who mutinies.

Mutinous – tending to mutiny.

Mutiny – an open revolt against constituted authority especially by sailors and soldiers against their officers

Mc

McKay, Clyde – mutineer on the SS Columbia Eagle – March 1970 Mutiny on an American ship during the Vietnam War. Lead by him and Alvin Glatkowski

N

Nore – 1793, one of 16 ships on the Channel Fleet, whose crew mutinied demanding a pay raise. One of the lead mutineers was Richard Parker.

P

Press Gang a group of people who are comissioned to force other men into military services.

S

San Antonio – ship captained by Juan DeCartegna.

Spithead - one of 16 ships on the Channel Fleet, whose crew mutinied demanding a pay raise. One of the lead mutineers was Richard Parker. 16 April – 15 May 1797

SS Columbia Eagle – March 1970 Mutiny on an American ship during the Vietnam War. Lead by Clyde McKay and Alvin Glatkowski

Maps

will be added per the request and special requirements of the instructor.

Artistic renderings

will be added per the request and special requirements of the instructor.

Bibliography

The following is a list of books that I have referenced throughout my research for all of the volumes contained within the MATH collection: More will be added in future publications.

#

20.000 Leagues under the Sea by Jules Verne 1962

A

A Guide to Shipwreck Sites along the Oregon Coast by Victor C. West 1984

A Mariner's Guide to Radiofacsimile Weather Charts by Dr. Joseph M. Bishop 1994

Atlas of Hawaii by Juvik and Juvik

B

Basic Hawaiiana 1990

C

Common Seashore Life of Southern California by Joel Hedgpeth and Sam Hinton 1961

Cruising Guide to California's Channel Islands by Brian Fagan 1983

D

Directory of Historical Repositories in Hawaii

Diver's Almanac Hawaii by Rock Baker

E

Emma Naca Rooke (1836 – 1885 Beloved Queen of Hawaii by Russell E. Benton

F

Feathered Gods and Fishhooks by Patrick Vinton Kirch 1985

Folk Wisdom of Hawaii by Ann Kondo Corum

G

Ghost Dog and Other Hawaiian Legends by George Thomas Armitage and Henry Pratt

Great Shipwrecks and Castaways Edited by Charles Neider 1989

Gulliver's Travels by Jonathan Swift 1999

H

Haunted Hawaiian Nights by Lopaka Kapanui 2005

Hawaii Museums and Cultural Attractions

Hawaiian Legends Index Vol 1 A-J

Hawaiian Legends Index Vol 2 K

Hawaiian Legends Index Vol 3 L – Y

Hawaiian Legends of Ghosts

Hawaiian Legends of Old Honolulu

Hawaiian Legends of Volcanoes

Hawaiian National Bibliography Vol I 1780 – 1830

Hawaiian National Bibliography Vol II 1831 – 1850

Hawaiian National Bibliography Vol III 1851 – 1880

Hawaiian National Bibliography Vol IV 1881 – 1900

Hawaiian Proverbs and Riddles by Henry Judd

History Makers of Hawaii A Biographical Dictionary A list of 500 people who have died that have contributed to Hawaii's History by Day A Grove

M

Mapping the lands and waters of Hawaii by Moffat & Fitzpatrick

Maps of the Ancient Sea Kings by Charles H. Hapgood 1979

Maui Mischevious Hero by Barbary Lyons 1969

Myths and Legends of Hawaii & Pacific

O

Oahu Revealed by Andrew Doughty 2011

Oceania Native Cultures of Australia and the Pacific Islands Vol I

Oceania Native Cultures of Australia and the Pacific Islands Vol II

P

Pele and Hiiaka A myth from Hawaii by Nathaniel Bright Emerson

Portland's Lost Waterfront by Barney Blacklock 2012

R

Robinson Crusoe by Daniel Defoe 1957

S

Sailing for Beginners by Moulton H. Farnham 1967

Schooner from Windward Two Centuries of Hawaiian Interisland Shipping by Thomas Liffin 1983

Sea and Earth: The Life of Rachel Carson by Phillip Sterling 1970

Seafaring Lore and Legend by Peter D. Jeans 2007

Silent Spring by Rachel Carson 1962

Silent World by Jacques-Yves Cousteau 1953

Solomon Mysteries by Marius Boirayan 2009

Supernatural Hawaii by Judi Thompson 2009

T

The Captain Encyclopedia by Robison

The Hawaiian Annotated Bibliography

The Hawaiian Canoe by Holmes

The Illustrated Atlas of Hawaii

The Journal of Captain James Cook III The Voyage of the Resolution and Discovery

The Life of Captain James Cook by John Cawte Beaglehole 1974

The Living Sea by Jacques-Yves Cousteau 1963

The Menehune of Polynesia and other mythical little people of Oceania by Katherine Luomala

The Night Marchers by Hoyt

The Riddle of the Bermuda Triangle Edited by Martin Ebon 1975

The Seaworthy Offshore Sailboat by John Vigor 2001

The United States Power Squadron Boating Course 2004

The Visual Encyclopedia of Nautical Terms Under Sail by Crown Publishers, New York 1978

Treasure Island by Roubert Louis Stevenson 1980

Two Years Before the Mast by Richard Henry Dana 1995

V

Vaka Moana Voyages of the Ancestors by K.R. Howe

Vikings of the Sunrise (Vikings of the Pacific) by Sir Peter Henry Buck 1985

Voyages to Hawaii before 1860

W

Who's Who in Pacific Navigation by Dunmore

Back Page

For further sources and information on the research conducted on this topic, it is recommended that you order the supplemental materials entitled notes and photos.

www.ingramcontent.com/pod-product-compliance
Lightning Source LLC
Chambersburg PA
CBHW081546280526
45788CB00010B/3366